Michael,
Enjoy
a pun-derful holiday!
[signature]

The BEST Christmas Pun & Dad Joke Book

201 Hysterical Holiday Puns +
301 Wildly Funny Everyday Puns
= 502 Hilarious Puns & Jokes!

By L. Newkirk

Nuhawk

Nuhawk LLC

x

1

Published in the United States of America

ISBN: 978-1-7379340-0-4

Edited by Laurie Newkirk and William Newkirk
Cover, Book Design and Art by Vincent Legg
Super Proofing by Barbara Wilkov

Photographers / Artists: Adobe Stock-Evergreen Border by
Postproduction / Adobe Stock-Christmas Ball by snake3d / Adobe
Stock-Snow by Tati Dsgn / Adobe Stock-Red Sign with Santa Hat
by vectorfusionart / Adobe Stock-Snowy Scene by Jittiwan / Adobe
Stock-Wrapped Presents by wetzkaz / Adobe Stock-Christmas Balls
Border by tilialucida / Adobe Stock-Ship Wheel by Creative-Touch /
Adobe Stock-Golf Ball by omphoto / Adobe Stock-Christmas Orna-
ment Icons by thebeststocker / Adobe Stock-New Years Eve Balloons
by Icons-Studio / Adobe Stock-New Years Bottle by Salamatik / Adobe
Stock-New Years Hat by Jemastock / Adobe Stock-Santa by Alien Cat
/ Adobe Stock-Toaster by Elala 9161 / Adobe Stock-Monkey by June
Yap / Adobe Stock-Cat by Klyaksun / Adobe Stock-Door by Layerform
/ Adobe Stock-Wreath by Luckygraphics / Adobe Stock-Snowman
by Jewjew / Adobe Stock-House Gear Icons by A Oleksii /
Grouch Marx by Vincent Legg

Published by Nuhawk, LLC
1117 Putnam Avenue, Suite 248, Riverside CT 06878

TABLE OF CONTENTS

Christmas Puns. 6

Christmas Riddles 42

Christmas Knock Knock Jokes 46

New Year's Puns 48

Puns on Puns 52

Celebrity Puns. 54

Dad Jokes for Older Dads 58

Everyday Puns. 62

Animal Puns 72

Car Puns 82

Food Puns 84

Music Puns 88

Work Puns. 92

Science & Technology Puns 100

Sports Puns 106

Christmas Puns...

Why doesn't Santa like small rooms?
He is claus-trophobic.

What did Santa use to help him walk when he twisted his ankle?
A candy cane.

What's a foot doctor's favorite thing about Christmas?
Mistle toe.

What happened when Frosty the Snowman got upset?
He had a melt down.

Why is a broken drum the best Christmas present?
You can't beat it!

Which of Santa's reindeer has the worst manners?
Rude-olph.

What did Santa Claus say to his wife about the weather?
It looks like rein, deer.

Why is Rudolph so good at answering trivia questions?
He nose a lot.

What's a chicken farmers favorite thing about Christmas?
Egg-nog.

What's the favorite Christmas carol of new parents?
Silent Night.

5

Christmas Puns...

How does Yoda know when Santa is around?
He can feel his presents.

Why is it difficult to make plans with Santa's reindeer?
They're flighty.

Why did the boy's grades drop after Christmas?
Because everything was marked down!

What did the elves say when Santa took attendance?
Present! Present!

Why do mummies like Christmas?
There's so much wrapping.

 **What is the best laundry detergent at Christmas?**
Yule Tide.

 **What did the sheep sing to his wife on December 25th?**
All I want for Christmas is Ewe.

 What did Frosty say when The Grinch was sneaking around?
He's up to snow good!

 What did Santa Claus say to the comic who made him laugh so hard?
You sleigh me.

 What did the cat think of Christmas?
It's Purr-fect.

Christmas Puns...

 What do you call Frosty when he works on his stomach muscles?
The Abdominal Snowman.

 What does Kris Kringle use to clean his hands?
Santa-tizer.

 **What do snowmen eat for breakfast?**
Frosted Flakes.

 What does Santa eat for breakfast?
Cheer-ios.

 **What did the salt & pepper say to the rosemary & basil on Christmas?**
Season's greetings.

 **How do we know the Grinch was born a pessimist?**
His blood type is B - (Be negative).

 How do we know Santa was born an optimist?
His blood type is B+ (Be positive).

 What did Santa's helpers study in kindergarten?
The Elf-abet

 What do you call a group of chess players bragging about their wins in a hotel lobby?
Chess nuts boasting in an open foyer.

 When Santa's helpers go to the store, how do they shop so fast?
They use the elf-checkout lane.

Christmas Puns...

 **What did Santa say when his helper Hermie finally became a successful dentist?**
He's an elf-made man.

 What time did the elf go visit Hermie the dentist?
Tooth-hurty (2:30).

 What song do Santa's helpers like?
Have Your Elf a Merry Little Christmas!

 Why do hip snowmen live in the North Pole?
It's cool.

 Why does the Christmas alphabet have only 25 letters?
It has no L (Noel).

How did Charlie Brown feel after Linus put his blanket around the little pine?
Tree-mendous!

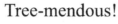

What did the valley girl say when she was asked if she liked the Christmas tree?
Fir-sure!

How do sheep say Merry Christmas?
Fleece Navidad!

What did the Christmas tree say when he started to cry at the end of the movie *It's a Wonderful Life*?
I'm getting sappy.

What did the Gingerbread Man say to the sad fruitcake?
What's eating you?

Christmas Puns...

What happened to the man who stole an Advent Christmas Calendar?
He got 25 days.

What did Frosty call it when he threw a big party?
A snow ball.

What did the man say when he raised his glass at Christmas dinner?
It's the most wine-derful time of the year.

What did the Buddhist want for Christmas?
Not the past, nor the future but the present.

Where did the farmer buy a Christmas gift for his pig?
Hamazon.

What are elves' favorite type of music?
Wrap.

What did Frosty's girlfriend do when she was mad at him?
She gave him the cold shoulder.

How do snowmen travel around?
By icicle.

What did Frosty say after watching Star Trek?
I want to boldly go where snowman has gone before.

What is Santa's favorite James Dean movie?
Rebel without a Claus.

Christmas Puns...

 Where did Frosty the Snowman keep his money?
In a snow bank.

 **What did the science teacher say to his fiancé while they were putting up Christmas decorations?**
We have great Chemis-tree.

 **What song and dance does Beyonce like to perform at Christmas?**
All the Jingle Ladies!

 What do reindeer use to decorate their antlers?
Hornaments.

 **What do you call a reindeer ghost?**
A carib-boo!

Why did the cat give everyone a gag gift for Christmas?
He was kitten around.

Who is never hungry at Christmas?
The turkey because he is always stuffed.

How did the man who collects snow globes feel at Christmas?
A little shaken.

Why is Christmas so cold?
Because it's in Decemberrrrr!

What kind of frog loves Christmas?
A mistle-toad.

Christmas Puns...

 Who delivers presents to cats at Christmas?
Santa Claws.

 What did the wife say to her husband who was a struggling Christmas tree farmer?
You need to branch out.

 **What did one Christmas ornament say to the other?**
Let's hang out.

 How do fairy tale books for reindeer end?
And they lived happily ever antler.

 What did the dog say to Santa on Christmas?
Happy Howl-idays!

What do cats say on Dec 25th?
Meow-y Christmas!

What did the English teacher call Santa's little helpers?
Subordinate clauses.

Where do Santa's reindeer stop for coffee?
Star-bucks.

Why did the Christmas tree go to the dentist?
He needed a root canal.

What do snowmen eat for lunch?
Iceberg-ers.

Christmas Puns...

 What did the Christmas tree farmer say to his wife while she was away?
I'm pining for you.

 What kind of motorcycle does Santa ride?
A Holly Davidson.

 **Why did no one bid on Donner and Blitzen on ebay?**
They were two deer.

 What would you call one of Santa's helpers who won the lottery?
Welfy.

 Why does Santa like going down chimneys?
It soots him.

What did the man drink to help him fall asleep at Christmas?
Egg-Nod.

Why is Santa Claus good at karate?
He has a black belt.

Why do reindeer wear bells?
Their horns don't work.

What do angels say to greet each other?
Halo there.

Who is Santa's favorite actor?
Willem Dafoe-ho-ho.

Christmas Puns...

Where do reindeer go if they lose a tail?
The retail store.

How did Scrooge win the football game?
The Ghost of Christmas passed.

Why did the band ask the turkey to join them?
They liked his drumsticks.

My friend just won the tallest Christmas tree competition...
...how do you top that?

Why did Santa go to the liquor store?
He wanted to lift his holiday spirits.

What is Santa's favorite potato chip?
Kringles.

What do you get when you cross Santa with a duck?
A Christmas quacker.

Why should Christmas dinner be well done?
So you can say, Merry Chrispness!

How do older people feel at Christmas?
Santa-mental.

Why did the Gingerbread Man go to the doctor?
He was feeling crummy.

Christmas Puns...

What kind of money do you use at the North Pole?
Cold cash.

What did the logger say when it was time to lift the Christmas pine?
One, two, tree.

What does a kitten on the beach get on Christmas morning?
Sandy Claws.

What does Santa use to go fishing?
His north pole.

What do you call it after all the Christmas presents have been opened?
A Christmess.

What do you call Santa when he has no change?
Saint Nickel-less.

What do you call it when Santa's helpers take a picture with their phone?
An elfie!

What does a snake sing at Chrismas?
Sssssssssssilver Bells!

Who is Santa's favorite singer?
Elf-ish Presley.

What's a vegan's favorite Christmas carol?
Soy to the World!

Christmas Puns...

Why does Santa's sleigh get such good mileage?
It has long-distance runners on each side.

What is Santa's tax status?
Elf-employed.

How did Santa get lost on Christmas Eve?
He got mis-sled.

How do Christmas trees get dressed up for a party?
They spruce up.

What do you use to decorate a canoe for Christmas?
Oar-naments.

What is Santa's favorite sandwich?
Peanut butter and jolly.

Who did Rudoph invite to his party?
His nearest and deer-est friends.

What did Dorothy from
***The Wizard of Oz* say to Santa?**
There's s(no)w place like home.

**What candy did the elves give Santa
to help his breath smell good?**
Orna-mints.

**Where do the best Christmas
singers live?**
In North or South Carol-ina.

Christmas Puns...

What did the doctor tell the Gingerbread Man to do for his sore knee?
Try icing it.

Why do basketball players leave cookies for Santa?
So he can dunk them.

Who should sing the National Anthem at a football game on Christmas Day?
A "wreath" a Franklin.

What do you get when you cross a famous archer with a gift-wrapper?
Ribbon Hood.

What season is the most successful?
WIN-ter!

What did Frosty the Snowman eat for breakfast?
Ice Crispies.

What did the beaver say to the Christmas tree?
Nice gnawing you.

Which dinosaur loves Christmas the most?
Tree Rex.

What's Tarzan's favorite Christmas song?
Jungle Bells.

What do you call a Christmas romantic comedy movie about bread?
Loaf Actually (Love Actually).

Christmas Puns...

 **What is a lamb's favorite Christmas carol?**
Have Yourself a Mary Little Christmas!

 What's the Grinch's least favorite band?
The Who.

 **What Christmas carol is heard in the desert?**
O Camel Ye Faithful!

 What do fish sing at Christmas time?
Christmas corals.

 Which U.S. state is Santa's favorite?
Idaho-ho-ho.

**What do you get if you cross
Saint Nicholas with a detective?**
Santa Clues.

**How does Saint Nicholas measure
his sleigh?**
In Santa-meters.

**What Olympic sport do Christmas
elves compete in?**
North Pole-vaulting.

What are Santa's helpers allergic to?
Sh-Elf-ish.

**Why did the elf put his bed next to
the fireplace?**
So he could sleep like a log.

Christmas Puns...

What kind of car does an elf drive?
A Toy-ota.

What do elves cook with?
Utinsels.

What did Santa give his reindeer who had an upset stomach?
Elk-a-seltzer.

Where do Santa's reindeer stop for ice cream when their job is done?
Deery Queen.

Did Rudolph go to school?
No, he was elf-taught.

What do snowmen wear on their heads?
Ice caps.

Why does Frosty the Snowman eat at Taco Bell?
He likes the chili.

How does Darth Vader enjoy his Christmas turkey?
On the dark side.

Why is Scrooge so nice to Santa's reindeer?
He values every buck.

How do you lift a frozen car?
With a Jack Frost.

Christmas Puns...

Which rock band is the mistletoe's favorite?
Kiss.

What is a webmaster's favorite Christmas carol?
Oh.com all ye faithful!

What three phrases best sum up the Christmas season?
"Peace on Earth," "Goodwill to Men," and "Batteries not Included."

Why is Santa a good race car driver?
Because he's always in the pole position.

What is Santa's favorite candy?
Jolly Ranchers.

What did the chef say on Christmas?
Let there be peas on earth.

Why did Scrooge not eat at the Italian restaurant?
The food cost a pretty penne.

What do snowmen call their offspring?
Chill-dren.

How do you feel when you cannot open your Advent Calendar Christmas chocolate?
Foiled.

Who hides at a bakery at Christmas?
A mince spy.

Christmas Puns...

Who does Santa call when his sleigh brakes down?
The Abominable Towman.

What would Santa say if he was a pirate?
Yo ho ho.

Where do they film movies about Christmas trees?
Holly-wood.

Who delivers presents to dogs at Christmas?
Santa Paws.

How does Santa take a picture?
With a pole-oriod camera.

What did the lawyer say when the elves were defending the shape of their ears?
They make some good points.

What Christmas carol did the cat in love sing to the other cat?
All I Want for Christmas is Mew.

What are dogs' favorite Christmas carols?
Deck the Halls with Bows on Collies, and Dachshund Through the Snow.

Why was the snowman looking through the carrots at the grocery store?
He was picking his nose.

What do unicorns use on top of their wrapped presents?
Rain-bows.

Christmas Puns...

What do grizzly bears drape on their Christmas trees?
Grrrr-lands.

What did the ghost sing to Santa Claus?
I'll Have a Boo Christmas Without You.

Why did Santa Claus get a ticket on Christmas Eve?
He left his sleigh in the Snow Parking Zone!

Who guards Santa's book collection?
Elf on a shelf.

What is the Lone Ranger's favorite Christmas carol?
Hi-Ho-Silver Bells.

**Why did the Winter Warlock do
so well in English class?**
He was the best spell-er.

**What did Scrooge call a cricket
at Christmas?**
A bah-um-bug.

**What do you get if you eat shiny
Christmas tree decorations?**
Tinselitis.

Why is Santa such a good gardener?
He likes to hoe, hoe, hoe.

Why is the Grinch such a good gardener?
He has a green thumb.

Christmas Puns...

 What do you get when you cross a snowman with a vampire?
Frostbite.

 What did Rudolph do on the scary roller coaster ride?
He held on for deer life.

 What do gingerbread men sleep on?
Cookie sheets.

 **Where does Santa keep his clothes?**
In his Claus-et.

 How much did Santa pay for his sleigh?
Nothing, it was on the house.

Christmas Riddles...

Where does Christmas come before Thanksgiving?
In the dictionary.

I can travel the world like Santa Claus without ever leaving my corner, what am I?
A stamp.

If the end of the year is December, what is the end of Christmas?
The letter "S."

I fall in the North Pole but never get hurt, what am I?
Snow.

What bites but doesn't have any teeth?
Frost.

Which reindeer is an astronaut's favorite?
Comet.   .

Which two letters describe Santa's bag after Christmas?
M, T.

What has a lot of needles but can't sew?
A Christmas tree.

Why did the Christmas tree go to the barber?
It needed to be trimmed.

What do you get if you cross a Christmas tree with an ipad?
A pine-Apple   .

Christmas Riddles...

If eleven elves were in the workshop and another joined them, what would he be?
The twelf.

What did the bald man say when he was given a comb for Christmas?
Thanks, I'll never part with it.

If athletes get athlete's foot, what do astronauts get?
Missletoe.

What is the most festive herb?
Christmas thyme.

How many presents can Santa put in an empty sack?
Just one, after that it's not empty.

What type of key do you need to put on a Nativity play?
A don-key.

How much does it cost to run Santa's sleigh?
Eight bucks, or nine if the weather is bad (Rudolph joins.)

How is a reindeer like a coin?
It has a head on one side and a tail on the other.

What's the difference between the North Pole and the South Pole?
All the difference in the world.

What do you call it when someone can predict what's inside a wrapped present?
A gift.

Christmas Knock Knock Jokes...

196

Knock, knock!   Who's there?

Ho Ho!   Ho Ho who?

Your Santa Claus impression needs work.

Knock, knock!   Who's there?
Ya!   Ya who?
I'm glad you're so excited about Christmas.

Knock, knock!   Who's there?
Anna!   Anna who?
Anna Partridge in a Pear Tree.

Knock, knock!   Who's there?
Santa!   Santa, who?
Santa you a Christmas card. Did you get it?

Knock, knock!   Who's there?
Elf!   Elf who?
Elf I knock again will you let me in?

Knock, knock! -   Who's there?
Murray!   Murray who?
Murray Christmas!

New Year's Jokes...

Why do you need a jeweler on New Year's Eve?
To ring in the New Year.

Every New Year's Eve, I look forward to a good show at Time's Square...
...and year after year, they drop the ball.

Where did the math lover want to be on New Year's Eve?
Times Square.

My New Year's resolution was to read more...
...so I turned on the subtitles on my TV.

My New Year's resolution is to stop procrastinating...
...but I'll wait until tomorrow to start.

What happens when you search the internet on how to light fireworks?
It comes up with dozens of matches.

I was going to quit all my bad habits for the new year...
...but then I remembered that nobody likes a quitter.

What was Dr. Frankenstein's New Year's resolution?
To make new friends.

What was the headline when Dracula passed out at midnight on New Year's Eve?
There was a count down.

Why did the man stand on one leg on New Year's Eve?
To start the new year on the right foot.

New Year's Jokes...

Why did the man take out the bread at midnight on December 31st?
He wanted to make a New Year's Eve toast.

What was the caterpillar's New Year's resolution?
To turn over a new leaf.

What did the girlfriend say when she was offered a raisin on New Year's Eve?
No thanks. I already have a date.

My dad gave up smoking cold turkey for New Year's, he's doing better now, but...
...he's still coughing up feathers.

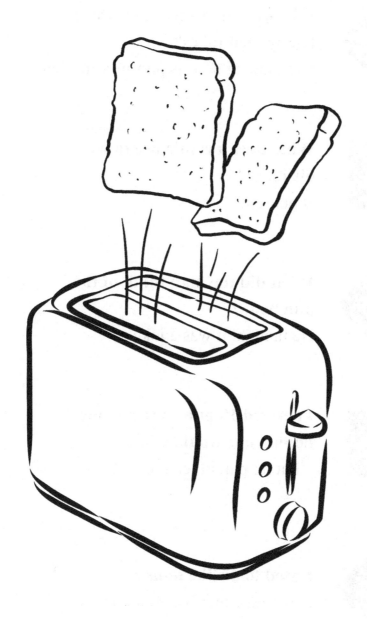

Puns on Puns...

 Why did the woman love the guy telling Dad jokes?
She thought he was pun-in-a-million.

 What does a comic use to write his jokes?
A pun-cil.

 What did the man think of the pun book?
He thought it was a joke.

 I entered 10 puns into a contest hoping one would win...
...but no pun in ten did.

 I used to dislike puns...
...but now they've groan on me.

 **Why did the comic do so well in English class?**
He was good at pun-ctuation.

 What happened when the comic stole another comic's joke?
He got a pun-ishment.

 Why do kleptomaniacs have a hard time understanding puns?
Because they take things literally.

 Someone told me a pun about maize...
...it was the corniest thing I've ever heard.

 **How did the man who told Dad Jokes refer to his new baby?**
As his pun-dle of joy.

Celebrity Puns...

 What did Jay-Z call his wife before they got married?
Feyonce (Fiancé.)

 Which actor is the best at hairdressing?
Harry Styles.

 Which celebrity is best at cutting down trees?
Justin Timber-lake.

 What do famous horses eat?
Matthew McConaug-HAY.

 Which coffee is most famous?
Ariana Grande.

Do you think Daniel Radcliff would ever play a Hobbit?
No, but Elijah Would.

How do you find Will Smith in the snow?
Look for Fresh Prints.

Which celebrity is best at fixing things?
Shawn Mendes.

What type of computer do Grammy winning singers use?
A Dell (Adelle.)

Who is a volleyball player's favorite director?
Spike Lee.

Celebrity Puns...

Today I found out that Dwayne Johnson lives in the apartment above mine...
...all these years I've been living under a Rock.

What would people call Whoopi Goldberg if she married Scooby-Doo?
Whoopi Doo!

What did Arnold Schwarzenegger say when he was invited to a music costume party?
I'll be Bach!

What did tennis player John McEnroe say when he went to space?
You cannot be Sirius!

Why are celebrities so cool?
They have a lot of fans.

What did Renée Zellweger say to the botanist?
You had me at aloe.

What is Serena Williams' favorite number?
10 is! (tennis.)

What did the man say about the sad Harrison Ford?
I've never seen Han so low.

How does Top Gun star Tom like to travel?
On a Cruise!

What do you call it when Steve Harvey and his wife argue?
A Family Feud.

Dad Jokes for Older Dads...

 What playwright was intimidated by Christmas?
Noel Coward.

 Who was the most positive comedian?
Bob Hope.

 Which comic is most comfortable on Halloween?
Red Skel-e-ton.

 What is the difference between a hippo and a Zippo?
One is heavy and the other is a little lighter.

 What is Fonzie's favorite letter?
Aaaaaaa!

Where did Farrah wash her hair?
Under the faucet.

Someone stole my mood ring yesterday...
...I still don't know how I feel about that.

**What do you get when you cross
Orson Wells with a heron?**
Citizen Crane.

What is an owl's favorite TV show?
Doctor Who.

**What do good elderly hockey
players get?**
Geri-hat-tricks.

Dad Jokes for Older Dads...

 Why did Groucho do well in school?
He got good Marx.

 Where do they search if someone loses something in a nursing home?
They search every nook and granny.

 Why did the man think 1970s solo female singers were vain?
He thought they were a bunch of pre-Madonnas.

 I just saw an elderly man help a youngster who was staring into his phone...
...to cross the street.

 What kind of pants did weightlifters wear in the 1970s?
Bar-bell bottoms.

Everyday Puns...

 What happened when the man went shopping for a pair of camouflage pants?
He couldn't find any.

 My friend was hit on the head with a can of soda.
Luckily, it was a soft drink.

 Why did the scarecrow get an award?
He was outstanding in his field.

What do you call a pencil with two erasers?
Pointless.

What did the man say about the book on anti-gravity?
I just can't put it down.

266

What's the difference between a duck and George Washington?
One has a bill on his face, and the other has his face on a bill.

267

Why did the woman get rid of her vacuum cleaner?
It was just gathering dust.

268

What do you call a coffee maker with a sixth sense?
Déjà brew

269

Why did the man say he excelled at sleeping?
He could do it with his eyes closed.

270

What do you call a wizard who's good with ceramics?
Harry Pottery.

Everyday Puns...

271 **What did the man say about the book on coins?**
I can't make heads or tails of it.

272 **Why was the tourist disappointed seeing the Liberty Bell?**
It wasn't all it was cracked up to be.

273 **Why did the woman think shopping centers were boring?**
Once you've seen one, you've seen them mall.

274 **Why didn't the skeleton have a phone?**
He had no body to talk to.

275 **Why did the team of witches keep losing the baseball games?**
Their bats kept flying away.

276 What was the elevator operator's view on life?

It has its up and downs.

277 Why do comics like to tell jokes about elevators?

They work on so many levels.

278 Why did the kleptomaniac give up stealing?

He couldn't take it anymore.

279 Why do math books make people sad?

They are filled with problems.

280 What do you call a monster with a high IQ?

Frank-Einstein.

Everyday Puns...

 What lies at the bottom of the sea and shivers?
A nervous wreck.

 What do you call a nice person from Sweden?
A Sweedie.

 Why shouldn't you trust atoms?
They make up everything.

 I'm not sure what the best thing about Switzerland is...
...but the flag is a big plus.

 How are relationships a lot like algebra?
Sometimes, you look at your X and wonder Y.

286 Why is the shovel such a great invention?
It was groundbreaking.

---

287 What did the man say when the clown held the door open for him?
What a nice jester!

---

288 Why did the man not like pessimistic horses?
He didn't like neigh-sayers.

---

289 What did they say to the guy who invented Zero?
Thanks for nothing.

---

290 I told a joke on a Zoom meeting and no one laughed...
....it turns out I'm not remotely funny.

Everyday Puns...

291
What happened when the man sued the airline for misplacing his luggage?
He lost the case.

292
When I get into work I immediately hide...
...good employees are hard to find.

293
Where do rainbows go when they're bad?
Prism.

294
What's made of leather and sounds like a sneeze?
A shoe.

295
Why are your fingers the most reliable part of the body?
You can always count on them.

296

I don't want to brag, but I finished the puzzle in under a week...
...and it said 2-4 years on the box.

297

The other day, my wife asked me to pass her lipstick, but I accidentally passed her a glue stick...
...she still isn't talking to me.

298

Why did the pirate go on holiday?
He was in serious need of some Aaaaaar and Aaaaaaar.

299

What happens when a red ship and a blue ship collide?
Everyone ends up marooned.

300

I can't stand jokes about insects...
...they really bug me.

Everyday Puns...

 Why did it take so long for the pirates to learn the alphabet?
They got stuck at C.

My wife accused me of being immature...
...I told her to get out of my fort.

 What building has the most stories?
A library.

I only catch cold on weekdays...
...probably because I have a weekend immune system.

Did you hear about the soap-stealing robber?
He decided to come clean.

306 How much do dead batteries cost?
Nothing, they are free of charge.

307 Did you hear about the woman who couldn't stop collecting magazines?
She had issues.

308 Why did the invisible man turn down the job offer?
He couldn't see himself doing it.

309 What did the man do who was afraid of elevators?
He took steps to avoid them.

310 Why shouldn't you eat a clock?
It's too time-consuming.

Animal Puns...

311

Why did the policeman arrest the bird?
He was a robin.

312

Why couldn't the pony sing in the choir?
He was a little horse.

313

What did the Dalmatian say after dinner?
That hit the spot!

314

Why didn't the lion eat the clown?
He thought he'd taste funny.

315

Why shouldn't you play poker with jungle cats?
Too many cheetahs.

316 Why didn't the leopard enjoy playing hide and seek?
Because he was always spotted.

317 What do you call a pig that does karate?
A pork chop.

318 How did the frog make such good beer?
He had lots of hops.

319 Why did the owl keep getting invited to parties?
He was such a hoot.

320 What do you call a crocodile detective?
An investi-gator.

Animal Puns...

321 Why did the elephant leave the circus?
It was sick of working for peanuts.

322 Where do mice park their boats?
At the hickory dickory dock.

323 Why does a chicken coop only have two doors?
Because if it had four doors then it would be a chicken sedan!

324 Why did Donald Duck not like the doctor?
He thought he was a quack.

325 What did the cat say when someone stepped on his paw?
Me-ow!

326 Why didn't the woman want to take her puppy for a walk?
She was dog tired.

327 Why did the woman not want to own a horse?
She thought she would be saddled with troubles.

328 What is a crab's favorite dog?
Doberman-pincher.

329 What do you call it when a kitten ruins the furniture?
A cat-astropy.

330 Where do bugs get off the train?
At the infestation.

Animal Puns...

331 Why did the man name his dogs Rolex and Timex?
They are watchdogs.

332 What do you call a bug that gets anxious before biting someone?
A nervous tick.

333 Why are frogs so happy?
They eat what's bugging them.

334 How do bees fix their hair?
With honey-combs.

335 What is the least sweaty bug?
Deoder-ant.

336 Why did the woman give her husband a squirrel as a present?
She thought he was nuts.

337 What do you call a penguin in the desert?
Lost.

338 Why is a frog not good on a jury?
He is always jumping to conclusions.

339 What's a monkey's favorite flower?
Chimp-pansy.

340 What's the king of the jungle's favorite flower?
Dandy-lion.

Animal Puns...

341 **Did you know there is a lot of hidden meaning in *The Lion King*?**
Yes, it's filled with Simba-lism.

342 **What kind of boat did the kitten want?**
A cat-a-maran.

343 **Why did the seagull fly over the sea?**
Because if he flew over the bay, he would be a bay-gull (bagel.)

344 **What do you call two monkeys who share an Amazon account?**
Prime-mates.

345 **Where did the cow go over the weekend?**
To the moo-vies.

346

Why do horses have low divorce rates?
They have stable relationships.

347

Why did the chicken go to the gym?
To work on his pecks.

348

How did the bee say the alphabet?
A, Me, C, D

349

Why do cows have hooves instead of feet?
Because they lactose.

350

What did the goose say when he purchased a new lipstick?
Put it on my bill.

Animal Puns...

351 **What do you call a flying primate?**
A hot air baboon.

352 **I have just started a dating website for chickens. It is not my normal job, I am just doing it...**
...to make hens meet.

353 **I taught my pet wolf how to meditate...**
...now he's aware wolf.

354 **How do you identify a dogwood tree?**
By its bark.

355 **What kind of dog does a magician have?**
A labracadabrador!

Car Puns...

356 **Why do comedians like jokes about tires?**
They get a lot of milage out of them.

357 **Why did the sad man buy a tire?**
He wanted to learn to roll with things.

358 **Why is Miss Piggy such a bad driver?**
She hogs the road.

359 **What did the road builder say when he made a mistake?**
Sorry, it's my own asphalt.

360 **What did the Goodyear store owner do when he turned 70?**
Went into re-tirement.

361 What's a race car driver's favorite meal of the day?
Brake-fast.

362 I couldn't remember how to do my seatbelt...
...but then it clicked.

363 What's the best car to drive underwater?
A Scub-aru.

364 What kind of car does a Jedi drive?
A To-yoda.

365 Why did the mechanic have to quit his job installing mufflers?
It was too exhausting.

Food Puns...

366 What do you say to an award-winning cheese maker?
Gouda job!

367 What do you call a fake noodle?
An impasta.

368 Why shouldn't you tell a legume chef your secrets?
They always spill the beans.

369 What is the saddest fruit?
Blue-berries .

370 What snack do people eat on the 4th of July?
Fire crackers.

371 Why was the lettuce always winning the race?
It was always a head.

372 What do you call a hen looking at lettuce?
Chicken-sees-a-salad.

373 My wife rearranged the labels on my spice rack...
...I haven't confronted her yet but the thyme is cumin.

374 What do you call friends you like to eat with?
Tastebuds.

375 Why couldn't the woman make orange juice?
She couldn't concentrate.

Food Puns...

376

I burnt my Hawaiian pizza last night...
...I should have cooked it on Aloha temperature.

377

I just learned that french fries are not from France at all...
...they were first cooked in Greece.

378

People often ask me how I smuggle chocolate into the movie theater...
...I have a few Twix up my sleeve.

379

Why did the man open a bakery?
He kneaded the dough.

380

What is the hot dog vendor's best-selling item on Oct 31st?
Hallo-weenies.

381 **What did The Buddha say to the hot dog vendor?**
Make me one with everything.

382 **What kind of food do you get when you cross a blizzard with a polar bear?**
A brrr-grrr! (burger.)

383 **How good was the joke about the watermelon?**
It was pitiful.

384 **Why didn't the comic tell the joke about the pizza?**
It was too cheesy.

385 **Where do rabbits go for breakfast?**
IHOP.

Music Puns...

386 **What do you call a music composer with problems?**
A trebled man.

387 **Why was music coming from the printer?**
The paper was jamming.

388 **Which legendary creature keeps musical time best?**
A metro-gnome.

389 **Why was the musician fired?**
The conductor found him too high-flute-in.

390 **Why was Mozart mad at his chickens?**
They kept saying, "Bach, Bach, Bach."

391 What is a pirate's favorite
instrument?
The guit-arrrr!

392 What do you call it when a jazz singer
spills a drink on his piano?
Ragtime.

393 Why was the piano laughing?
Because someone was tickling its ivories.

394 My friends and I are in a band
called "Duvet"...
...we're a cover band.

395 I asked a pianist if he could play the
"Chickpea Song." He said maybe...
...can you hummus a few bars?

Music Puns...

396 Why aren't tubas used in country bands?
Because they're heavy metal.

397 What music do frogs and rabbits like?
They both like hip-hop.

398 Why did the pianist keep banging his head against the keys?
He was playing by ear.

399 What is Beethoven's favorite fruit?
Ba-na-na-naaaaa.

400 What's the best kind of music to listen to when fishing?
Something catchy.

401 Why couldn't the string quartet find their composer?
He was Haydn.

402 Why didn't Handel go shopping?
Because he was baroque.

403 What do you call a group of musical whales?
An orca-stra.

404 What did the drummer name his daughters?
Anna one, Anna two!

405 I used to have an addiction to the Hokey Pokey...
...but then I turned myself around.

Work Puns...

406 How did the artist handle the bad review?
He brushed it off.

407 I told my doctor I broke my arm in two places...
...he told me to stop going to those places.

408 Why should you avoid artists?
They tend to be sketchy.

409 What is an accountant's view on life?
It has its pluses and minuses.

410 What did the farmer say when he started growing large pickles?
This is a big dill.

Why was the woman upset with the driving instructor?
She thought he was steering her wrong.

411

Why was the doctor's wife annoyed with him?
He kept needling her.

412

Why did the woman stop dating the vineyard owner?
He whined too much.

413

Why do nurses carry red crayons?
In case they needed to draw blood.

414

Why did Tarzan have a hard time at his job?
He couldn't get into the swing of things.

415

Work Puns...

416

What did the dummy say to the ventriloquist?

Stop putting words in my mouth.

417

Why did the woman and the shoemaker break up?

She thought he was a heel and he thought she had no sole.

418

What is an astronaut's favorite key on the keyboard?

Space bar.

419

Why did the astronaut move into a larger house?

He needed more space.

420

What was the tailor's issue with the pants?

They didn't seam right.

Why did the photographer quit his job?
He didn't like the way it was developing.

What did the clockmaker do when it was time to eat?
He washed his hands.

How did the surfer say goodbye?
He waved.

Why did the dentist stop talking to the woman?
Her comments were too biting.

What did the man say when he was fired from the rubber band factory?
I'll bounce back.

Work Puns...

426 Why did the train conductor stop dating the woman?

He couldn't keep track of her.

427 What does a train conductor like to do with bubble gum?

Choo-choo.

428 Why did the woman stop dating the accountant?

Nothing he said added up.

429 I went to a psychic and knocked on her front door. She yelled, "Who is it?"...

...so I left.

430 My wife dated a clown before she started going out with me...

...I had some pretty big shoes to fill.

431

My boss told me to have a good day...
...so I went home.

432

**Why did the woman stop being
an investment banker?**
She lost interest.

433

**As I get older, I think of all the people
I have lost along the way...**
...maybe a career as a tour guide
wasn't for me.

434

**I didn't think my chiropractor was
very good...**
...however, now I stand corrected.

435

**The man quit his job as a personal
trainer because the weights were
too heavy...**
...he turned in his too weak notice.

Work Puns...

436 **What did the eye doctor say to his son who had bad grades?**
I thought you'd be a better pupil.

437 **What happened to the archeologist who lost her job?**
Her career was in ruins.

438 **Why did the man quit being a barber?**
He couldn't cut it.

439 **What do attorneys wear in court?**
Lawsuits.

440 **What did the janitor say when he jumped out of the closet?**
Supplies!

441

Why did the man quit his job as a tailor?
He wasn't suited for it.

442

People are often shocked...
...when they find out what a bad electrician I am.

443

Why did the plumber have to quit his job fixing sinks and showers?
The work was just too draining.

444

Why do gardeners make good gossip columnists?
They know all the dirt.

445

What do you call a lazy physician?
Dr. Do Little.

Science & Technology Puns...

446

I took a rocket science course last year...
...it was a blast.

447

Did you hear what happened when Neil Armstrong first walked on the moon?
He didn't understand the gravity of the situation.

448

I wanted to buy the latest telescope so I could see outer space...
...but the cost was astronomical.

449

How many ears does Spock have?
Three...a left ear, a right ear and a final frontier.

450

How did the astronaut feel during his mission in space?
He was so happy, he was over the moon.

451 Why did the employee get fired from a keyboard factory?
He wasn't putting in enough shifts.

452 My friend just installed ethernet in his home in Australia...
...I can't wait to visit the LAN down under.

453 Where do you find boats online?
Google docks.

454 Why shouldn't you use the word sausage as your password?
It's the wurst.

455 Why do kids like going on the internet?
All the cookies!

Science & Technology Puns...

456 Why is Google like a submarine?
The problem starts when you open too many windows.

457 Did you hear about the restaurant on the moon?
The food was good but there was no atmosphere.

458 What do you get when you cross a computer with an alligator?
A mega-BYTE.

459 Where did the Google employee go to get a drink?
A search bar.

460 What did the computer programmer have as a snack?
Micro chips.

461

Why are some internet users so selfish?

It's all meme, meme, meme.

462

Why was the computer programmer late to work?

He had a hard drive.

463

Why did the spider use Google?

To find some good web-sites.

464

What happened to the plant in math class?

It grew square roots!

465

How does a tree cutter get into his computer?

He logs in.

Science & Technology Puns...

466

Why was the cat sitting near the computer?
He was watching the mouse.

467

Why didn't the man buy anything online through Google?
He was just browsing.

468

Somebody stole my Microsoft Office and they're going to pay...
...you have my Word.

469

What do you call security guards working outside Samsung stores?
Guardians of the Galaxy.

470

What do you get if you divide the circumference of a pumpkin by its diameter?
Pumpkin pi (π)!

Sports Puns...

471

What did Chewbacca win when he made it to the big leagues?
Wookiee of the Year.

472

There are so many statistics in baseball that the players are now...
...running around data bases.

473

What happened when the runner was afraid of hurdles?
He got over it.

474

Why did the golfer have an extra pair of pants with him?
In case he got a hole in one!

475

I couldn't figure out why the baseball kept getting larger...
...then it hit me.

476 What did the man say when he reached the top of the mountain?
It was a peak experience.

477 What do you call a runner's wedding that lasts a long time?
A marry-thon.

478 Did you hear about the ski trip?
It started out fine, but went downhill fast.

479 How many golfers does it take to change a lightbulb?
Fore!

480 What position do ghosts play in hockey?
Ghoul-tender.

Sports Puns...

What did the bowler think of the food?
It was right up his alley.

What kind of bar did the swimmer like?
A dive.

Why was the golfer sad?
He was going through a rough patch.

What do NFL football cheerleaders drink before they perform at a game?
Root beer!

Why are basketball players so messy when they eat?
They dribble a lot.

486 Why was the hockey player nervous about his relationship?
He knew he was on thin ice.

487 What did the football coach say to the broken vending machine?
Give me my quarterback.

488 Why can't football players wear glasses during the game?
It's a contact sport.

489 Why are figure skaters so relaxed?
They know how to let things slide.

490 How do football players handle their problems?
They tackle them head on.

Sports Puns...

Why do people watch soccer?
They get a kick out of it.

What did the baseball player say to the airline flight attendant?
Put me in coach!

What happened when the football coach's dog ran onto the field during a game?
He got called for ineligible retriever downfield.

Why couldn't the all-star player listen to music?
He broke all the records.

Why did the volleyball player bring a map and compass to the game?
She was working on her serve-vival skills.

496 Why are lacrosse players so succesful?
They are goal oriented.

497 Where do baseball players keep their mitts when they are driving?
In the glove compartment.

498 Why was the marching band so noisy?
They were trying to drum up some attention.

499 How do baseball players stay friends?
They touch base every once in a while.

500 Why are frogs such good baseball players?
They are good at catching flies.

Final Puns...

Why was Cinderella kicked off the soccer team?
She kept running away from the ball.

What did my Dad say about this book?
It's pun-derful!

I hope you found this book holly-larious and it filled your Christmas with tree-mendous laughter and cheer!

May you have a very Merry Christmas and a Happy New Year filled with joy, pun-believably great jokes...and a few groaners for good measure!
— L. Newkirk

Made in the USA
Middletown, DE
07 December 2024